1 MONT

FREE
READING

at

www.ForgottenBooks.com

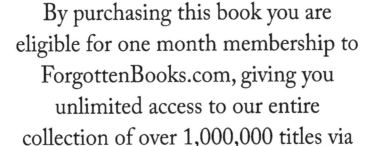

By purchasing this book you are
eligible for one month membership to
ForgottenBooks.com, giving you
unlimited access to our entire
collection of over 1,000,000 titles via
our web site and mobile apps.

To claim your free month visit:

www.forgottenbooks.com/free276671

ISBN 978-0-428-19607-3
PIBN 10276671

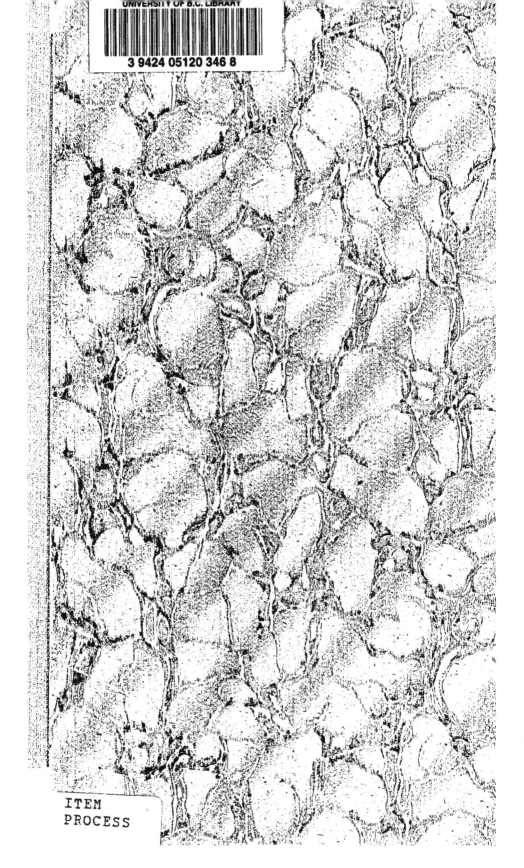

THE LIBRARY

THE UNIVERSITY OF
BRITISH COLUMBIA

CITY PLANNING

A COMPREHENSIVE ANALYSIS OF THE SUBJECT ARRANGED FOR THE CLASSIFICATION OF BOOKS, PLANS, PHOTOGRAPHS, NOTES AND OTHER COLLECTED MATERIAL

WITH ALPHABETIC SUBJECT INDEX

BY

JAMES STURGIS PRAY

CHAIRMAN, SCHOOL OF LANDSCAPE ARCHITECTURE,
HARVARD UNIVERSITY

AND

THEODORA KIMBALL

LIBRARIAN, SCHOOL OF LANDSCAPE ARCHITECTURE,
HARVARD UNIVERSITY

CAMBRIDGE
HARVARD UNIVERSITY PRESS
1913

) ÷

CITY PLANNING

A COMPREHENSIVE ANALYSIS OF THE SUBJECT ARRANGED FOR THE CLASSIFICATION OF BOOKS, PLANS, PHOTOGRAPHS, NOTES AND OTHER COLLECTED MATERIAL

WITH ALPHABETIC SUBJECT INDEX

BY

JAMES STURGIS PRAY

CHAIRMAN, SCHOOL OF LANDSCAPE ARCHITECTURE,
HARVARD UNIVERSITY

AND

THEODORA KIMBALL

LIBRARIAN, SCHOOL OF LANDSCAPE ARCHITECTURE,
HARVARD UNIVERSITY

CAMBRIDGE
HARVARD UNIVERSITY PRESS
1913

TABLE OF CONTENTS

PREFACE

The term City Planning is used to signify "the intelligent control and guidance of the physical conformation, growth, and alteration of cities, towns, or considerable parts thereof, considered in their entirety"; [1] or, more briefly, the organization of the physical city, town, or district to fit it to its complex use. It includes the planning of towns, suburbs, villages, and any considerable urban, suburban, or even intimately related rural districts. Material other than that embraced under the above definition is included in this outline only when the subject-matter is treated or considered as having a definite relation to the city plan or its elements. For the purposes of this classification, planning includes re-planning, and the two are regarded as virtually synonymous. Current usage sanctions three different meanings for the phrase city plan: first, the form of organization scheme, conception — purely subjective; second, the drawings, graphic expressions of this conception; third, the physical city resulting from the carrying out of this conception, the scheme realized; these two latter uses being strictly objective. We use the phrase in only the first of these senses, the subjective — the scheme or form of organization.

USEFULNESS OF THE CLASSIFICATION

That all the topics here included have been found necessary in order adequately to care for the arrangement of the ideas now current in city planning — whether expressed in literal or graphic language — is an impressive indication of not only the present magnitude of the subject of City Planning itself, but also the volume of thought already on record within this field. So far as we know, this is the first comprehensive, systematic setting forth of the scope and

[1] Professor Frederick Law Olmsted, Chairman of the National Conference on City Planning.

5

varied character of this field to such a scale. Yet, so clearly have the relations and scopes of the principal divisions here made of the subject now established themselves, and so far have we been dominantly influenced in choosing for main heads and subheads units of area and the objects upon them distinguished by function, that we believe no radical reorganization of this field is ever likely to occur, and that this classification, which has been prepared with unusual care and had already the helpful criticism of many minds representing many parts of the field, can be adopted with unusual assurance as to its usefulness for an indefinite time to come. Certain parts of the classification must, of course, be expanded from time to time as the corresponding parts of the subject develop. The numbering of the scheme allows for this expansion.

The approach to city planning to-day is still from many directions. The number of these directions, will, as time passes, increase rather than diminish; but, from whatever related, contributory, or overlapping field one comes to city planning, one cannot hope to grasp the problem of the city plan as a whole or the true relation of one's special field to it without reference to some such comprehensive and systematic analysis, expressed or implied, as is here presented. Moreover, however the directions of approach and hence the points of view differ, the organization of the modern city for health, efficiency, and beauty — not to say economy — remains essentially the same, and therefore such a comprehensive classification should be useful alike to the municipal official, the business administrator, the civil engineer, the sanitary expert, the transportation engineer, the housing reformer, the architect, and the landscape architect, as well as the representative of any one of various other special services, in proportion as his occupation enters and contributes to the field of city planning; and the index will show him quickly at what points his special material is provided for. Thus, to all who are concerned with city planning the classification aims to be useful either for the classification of collected material, for the indication of relations between special parts of the whole field, or for a comprehensive presentation and systematic analysis of the subject. In this last way, it is thought that the classification will be particularly useful to students of city planning in colleges and technical schools where the subject is to any extent taught.

There is much in the rapid spread of the city-planning movement to-day that is unintelligent, superficial, injurious to the best interests of those living and working in cities. It is hoped that such a comprehensive view and systematic handling as here given may help in some small measure to a more general rational conception of this vital field. However this may be, it is issued in response to a demand which has been expressed by practising city planners, city administrators, instructors and students, and librarians, as well as by professional men in the related fields already mentioned.

The very newness of city planning as an art, science, and profession renders the even development of a classification scheme impossible. Certain portions must be scarcely more than suggestive, but even here, in calling attention to the dearth of published material in particular sections of the subject, the classification scheme is useful in pointing out special fields of desirable research.

As the joint authorship of this city-planning classification implies, the principle has been recognized that, to be generally useful, any classification intended as this is to cover the arrangement both of ideas and of actual material, must be a compromise between a theoretical organization of the subject and an arrangement guided merely by existing material. If wholly the former, the classification will not be usable in libraries; while if based only on library needs, its services to those actively interested in city planning must be greatly diminished.

PRACTICAL APPLICATION OF THE CLASSIFICATION TO AR-
RANGEMENT OF EXISTING MATERIAL

The forms of material which might occur in a collection relating to city planning are: published literature, including books, pamphlets, reports, periodical articles, and clippings; graphic material, published or in original form, including maps, plans, drawings, photographs, plates, postcards, and miscellaneous pictorial matter; manuscript material, including notes and bibliographical references. All these forms of material are represented in the Library of the School of Landscape Architecture at Harvard, for which this City-planning Scheme was originally developed. In fact, the Scheme originated and has been worked out directly in connection with the organization of the extensive and rapidly growing collections on city planning in this Library.

In preparing one outline of the subject to cover material in such diverse forms, it is obvious that certain sections will be developed to provide more particularly for published literature and certain others more particularly for graphic material. In fact on certain topics given in the outline, perhaps nothing has been *written* at all, although there may be many photographs. The development of the scheme, therefore, while considerably in advance of the literature of the subject in parts, is yet proportionate in consideration of the total material covered.

The proportions of the scheme have furthermore been affected by the necessity to represent various points of view as well as various physical entities, and by the desirability of suggesting various possible arrangements. For the same material may often be arranged in a number of different ways to serve different objects, as shown by the following illustration: a lot of postcards representing residential streets in various industrial cities might be classified either in 1675, Residential districts, or 2235, Residential streets, or 5320, Industrial cities, according to the way in which the owner of these cards would wish to consult them. If he had three copies of each, they could be arranged in all three places. Such duplication is seldom possible, and people have to be content with cross-references. Manuscript notes offer much the same possibilities of arrangement as the postcards just given as an illustration, and may be handled with a similar flexibility. The value of the classification for the arrangement of notes is very great to those interested professionally in city planning and constantly collecting data. In connection with the use of the classification for notes, it is suggested that by making a check mark in the printed index to the classification whenever a topic is looked up to find the number to apply to the particular note in question, the user will have constantly an up-to-date index to the material he has already assembled. The use of the classification for arranging bibliographical references is also important. The authors have had continually in mind the use of this scheme for the arrangement of the extensive City-planning Bibliography in preparation by the School of Landscape Architecture in coöperation with the Library of Congress, of which a Check List appeared in the May, 1912, issue of the magazine "Special Libraries." As stated in the Prefatory Note, and also at the end of the Check List, where a summary tentative outline was offered, the Harvard City-planning Scheme has been officially adopted by the Library of Congress for the classification of titles in the City-planning Bibliography.

THIS CLASSIFICATION IN RELATION TO OTHER CLASSIFICA-
TION SCHEMES

Library of Congress Classification

In looking about for a basis on which to construct a classification scheme for its special Library of Landscape Architecture, including City Planning, for which there was no adequate provision in any existing classification, the School of Landscape Architecture decided that it was wiser to choose one which could be related to some general scheme already worked out, that could care for whatever material in allied fields it should be desirable to have in the Library. Mr. Sidney Kimball, then Assistant in the School, made a study of existing classifications, on the basis of which the School decided to adopt the Library of Congress Classification, because it is comprehensive, generally known through the wide circulation of printed catalogue cards numbered according to it, and adapted in principle to serve as a basis for the arrangement of the special field of the Library. This principle is a combination of logical subdivision with convenient sequence, allowing a maximum of elasticity in development. Its simple sequential system of numbering was found easy to use in the Library, and convenient of application to the outline of the subject without forcing.

In correspondence with Mr. Charles Martel, then Chief Classifier of the Library of Congress, a place was assigned the subjects in the general Library of Congress scheme (in which no adequate provision for Landscape Architecture or City Planning existed) in Class N, Fine Arts. Landscape Architecture and City Planning were erected as independent sub-classes coördinate with and immediately following Architecture, numbered NA. As the sub-class designation NB was already in use, it was necessary to use a three-letter combination which would assume Architecture to be NA(A), Landscape Architecture NAB, and City Planning NAC. Although City Planning is not primarily a fine art its fundamental esthetic aspect and its close connection with the practice of Landscape Architecture and Architecture were considered to justify its position in class N.

If this City-planning Classification is to be used as a part of the general Library of Congress Classification Scheme — as it is used in the Library of the School of Landscape Architecture — only material included under City Planning in its stricter definition will be classed in NAC; all other material will go in the appropriate Library of Congress class, e. g., Land and Housing, HD; Transportation, HE; Architecture, NA(A); Public Health, RA; Roads and Pavements, TE; Building Laws, TH. This City-planning Classification Scheme will however be used by many people technically interested in city planning who wish to use it as a complete basis of arrangement for all the material which they may collect on the whole subject, including affiliated fields. Provision has therefore been made in this Scheme as it now stands for such a use, in connection with material on affiliated fields, with a reference in the more important cases, to the Library of Congress class where a fuller subdivision of the subject may be found. Those who find this Scheme full enough as it is may disregard these references entirely. Those who wish to go further may consult the Library of Congress classes referred to, the indexes in the backs of the "Schedules" containing these classes, and also the alphabetical list of subject headings published by the Library of Congress.

PREFACE

Forthcoming Landscape Architecture Classification

It is of interest to note the relation to this City-planning Scheme of the Landscape Architecture Scheme (NAB) in preparation by Professor Henry V. Hubbard and Theodora Kimball, of which a brief summary and adaptation appeared in the January, 1913, issue of the quarterly "Landscape Architecture." This forthcoming scheme will contain carefully worked-out cross-references to the City-planning Scheme, and each might well contain material not proper to the other according to the point of view; as, for instance, in the case of Parks, which in the City-planning Scheme are treated primarily as unit areas of a city and in the Landscape Architecture Scheme primarily as landscape compositions.

Adaptations to Other Systems of Classification

There appears to be no reason why this outline of the subject of city planning, very much as it stands, should not be used in connection with other systems of classification in general use. For instance, at present the Dewey Decimal Classification contains no special provision for city planning. The New York State Library states that section 710 in that system is the place where a city-planning sub-class might be developed. The decimal system of numbering might be applied to the outline of this City-planning Classfication somewhat as follows: .01–.08 *Bibliography* through *Museums*, .11–.17 *Collected Works* through *General Special* (or these form headings could be rearranged to conform with general decimal classification practice); .2 *City-planning movement;* .3 *Legislation;* .4 *Methods of technical procedure;* .5 *Study and teaching;* .6 *Composition of city plans;* .7 *Elements of city plans;* .8 *Types of city plans;* .9 *Geographical arrangement.* The subheads would be similarly numbered in decimal fashion so that a paper on, for instance, the economic aspects of city planning, might have for its classification number 710.623; or again an article on suburban station grounds, 710.71333. Of course some adjustments would have to be made, but the authors believe that the outline, as *an outline of the subject,* could stand.

PREFACE

Headings

It should be stated that the first series of main headings (see the Summary Outline) through 300, General special, have been selected from those in general use by the Library of Congress. They might be termed "form headings," since they refer particularly to the form in which the material appears, *e. g.*, a Periodical, a Dictionary. The phrase "General special" is used as a heading for material, which, though *general*, is not comprehensive but deals with some *special* phase of the general topic, *e. g.*, under the heading Conduits. Wires, the topic 2857, Relation to street maintenance, appears under General special. This heading has been used consistently throughout this scheme, sometimes with subheads, often alone, with a gap in the numbering to permit the insertion of future subheads if desired.

The second series of headings beginning with 500, City-planning movement, constitute a systematic subdivision of the field, adjusted to meet the demands of classifying material which, as physical objects, can stand in the files only in one place. Aspectual subdivisions, and provision for arrangement from different points of view, need not encumber the simplicity of the outline for use with graphic material representing objects alone. As has been stated earlier in this introduction, certain headings apply more to literature and certain others more to pictorial matter. Use of the topics will soon reveal this distinction. Certain subheads have been provided uniformly under all the principal elements; beyond this, an exact uniformity of phrase under all subheads has not been sought: it has seemed better to use whatever phrases were most expressive in the given instance.

However, as far as possible, corresponding parts of the outline itself have been constructed as uniformly as possible, to offer mnemonic advantage, for instance, under Vegetation, Special uses (4870), the topics have been arranged in the same order as the large headings under Elements.

In order to present the subject clearly, each major subdivision of the outline is developed to a certain proportion, even if the subheads are given only as cross-references, *e. g.*, Squares, 4400. In minor cases, however, only typical topics have been given under a heading, often in order to make clear the kind of material which should be classified there. These type subheads have been generally chosen because they represented actual existing material, *e. g.*, 1246, to cover a couple of recent magazine articles on the influence of aviation on the planning for total effect of the city as seen from above. Gaps have been left in the numbering for the insertion of similar subheads.

In arranging a series of subheads, a coherent sequence has been preferred to an alphabetic arrangement, on account of the advantage gained for pictorial material, as shown by section 3820+, Minor structures. In general, the sequence of the actual material as arranged by this scheme has been carefully considered.

Numbering

The numbering of the Scheme requires some explanation. The system is that employed by the Library of Congress, a sequence of simple cardinal numbers, with gaps left between the numbers assigned the topics given, in order to allow for the insertion of new topics. Further expansion may be provided for by the use of decimals, as in Library of Congress Class HD, section 9000+. The numbering of the City-planning Scheme has been done loosely, since the subject is growing so rapidly, and may develop at an unexpected point or in an unexpected way. Several hundred numbers have been left open to provide for such emergency. In classifying material in a library using the Library of Congress Classification, the numbers of the outline would be preceded by NAC, the general class designation for city planning. For a collection wholly on city planning and using only this scheme, NAC need not be used, since the numerical designation is sufficient. In a collection using the forthcoming Landscape Architecture Scheme (NAB) and this scheme (NAC), B might be used for Landscape Architecture and C for City Planning, or whatever mnemonic device the owner preferred.

Indentation

It has not been possible to express exact coördination and subordination of heads and subheads by the indentation. Often importance or bulk of material has pulled a logically subordinate topic into a more important place. Furthermore, indentation by exact logical arrangement would make many of the headings too far to the right of the page for convenient printing; and the insertion of headings to show theoretical relations, where not necessary for clearness, would render the outline clumsy for use in classifying material.

Explanatory Notes

Notes have been given throughout the scheme explaining the meaning of a heading and what material should be classified under it, wherever the authors felt these points were not self-evident.

Cross-references

Cross-references have been freely made between headings containing related material and further to call attention to headings under which the same material might be arranged from different points of view. In making these cross-references, where there has been no doubt as to the connection, the number referred to has alone been given without the corresponding heading. In doubtful cases, the heading referred to has been given in addition to the numerical reference. The authors do not feel that it was advisable to give referred-to headings except in doubtful cases, on account of the great increase in bulk which the headings for the very large number of cross-references would have caused. In making the numerical cross-reference to a topic, the initial number only has been used, followed by a plus sign (*e. g.*, 4300 +) if the topic occupies more than one number. Throughout the scheme the numbers and topics given in curves followed by a reference to some other number show where material might be classified if desired for some special purpose, but where the authors do not think it as well placed from a general point of view as under the number referred to. The Index may be used to supplement cross-references in the text.

PREFACE

Summary Outline

Besides the full Classification Scheme, the authors have included a Summary Outline, consisting of the main heads and subheads. This Summary serves to show the general construction of the Scheme, and also as a briefer basis for arrangement of material where there is only a small collection, or a collection developed at some one point, for which section alone the fuller scheme would be necessary. The topics given in the Summary Outline are printed in capitals in the full scheme, both for emphasis and to facilitate reference from the Summary to the Scheme itself.

Geographical Table

The Geographical Table given with this Classification was taken substantially from that included in Library of Congress Class N, called Table II. It is here numbered to use for the section City Planning, by special countries and cities. The same numbers (1–184) in the same relation, or these numbers as decimals, can be used at other points in the scheme where a geographical subdivision is desired. Appended to the Geographical Table is a careful explanation of the possible subarrangement of material under individual countries and cities.

Index

The alphabetic subject Index to this Classification has been made exceptionally full. The text of the Scheme has been indexed to bring out catch-words in many cases, as well as subjects, for the convenience of the person who remembers a word, phrase, or special form of heading and wishes to find it again. As few as possible "see" references have been made in the index: the numerical reference has been given for each significant word of a phrase, instead of a cross-reference (*e. g.*, Street name-plates, Name-plates, Street), unless there are subdivisions under the topic, in which case a "see" reference has had to be made to avoid excessive duplication in printing. The "see" references in the Index consist mostly of phrases not used in the Classification which might possibly be looked for in the index and under which reference is given to the sections in this Scheme relating to the subject. A word or phrase in curves, *e. g.*, Soil (Data), is given in many cases after an entry in the index to explain its bearing. It has been the intention of the authors that the Index shall be of the greatest possible service to users of the Classification, and all the means which have presented themselves have been employed to accomplish this object.

PUBLICATION OF PRELIMINARY OUTLINE

In May, 1913, when the classification was approaching completion, a Preliminary Outline was issued (Printed as Manuscript), in order to invite ·suggestion and criticism, before the full Scheme should be fixed in final form. This Outline contained merely the main headings, together with some indication of the material included thereunder, without numbers or index. The Outline was circulated widely both among librarians and among those professionally interested in the subject of City Planning, particularly members of the National Conference on City Planning, whose technical comment was awaited with interest. Meantime the authors had themselves been developing the fuller scheme to a point considerably beyond that represented by the published Preliminary Outline. Among the large number of acknowledgments and appreciations received from those to whom copies of the Outline were sent, very few contained constructive criticisms. Those suggestions and criticisms which were made were carefully considered and in every case acted upon.

ACKNOWLEDGMENTS

Professor Frederick Law Olmsted, Chairman of the National Conference on City Planning, who had been interested in the Scheme from its beginning and who had already given constructive suggestions, considered the Preliminary Outline and suggested valuable improvements, particularly in the sections relating to Data for City Planning, which now stand practically in accordance with the subdivisions he made in his address on the subject before the City-planning Conference, May, 1913. Mr. Flavel Shurtleff, Secretary of the Conference, who is making a special study of the legal aspects of city planning, made valuable suggestions for the

PREFACE

section Legislation while the Outline was in manuscript. Professor Charles W. Killam of the School of Architecture at Harvard is responsible for the classification under Types of Building Construction as it now appears. Among others, Mr. John Nolen of Cambridge, Professor James Ford of the Department of Social Ethics at Harvard, and Professors Brix and Genzmer of the K. Technische Hochschule, Berlin, have made suggestive comments. Mr. H. H. B. Meyer, Chief Bibliographer of the Library of Congress, whose connection with the forthcoming City-planning Bibliography gives him a particular interest in the Scheme, and who had approved it in its early stages for the arrangement of the Bibliography, also made several very valuable suggestions, which were incorporated.

Besides grateful acknowledgment to those already mentioned, the authors desire to make special acknowledgment to the following persons: to Mr. Sidney Fiske Kimball, then Assistant in the School of Landscape Architecture at Harvard University and now Instructor in Architecture at the University of Michigan, for the use of his draft for a tentative outline of classification for use in the School of Landscape Architecture Library, which made a most valuable basis for further development; to Mr. Charles Martel, then Chief Classifier and now Chief of the Catalogue Division of the Library of Congress, for his consideration of the scheme, in its early stages, in personal conference in March, 1912, and for his interpretation of the principles of the Library of Congress Classification as applying to this field; to Professor Henry V. Hubbard, of the School of Landscape Architecture at Harvard University for constructive thought and unstinted assistance in the development of the scheme throughout the undertaking.

JAMES STURGIS PRAY,
THEODORA KIMBALL.

CAMBRIDGE, MASS.,
November, 1913.

CITY-PLANNING CLASSIFICATION

SUMMARY OUTLINE

If used in connection with Library of Congress Classification, prefix NAC to numbers.

  0 Bibliography.

 (1) Periodicals.

 15 Yearbooks.

(20) Societies.

(40) Congresses. Conferences. Conventions.

(50) Exhibitions.

(70) Museums.

180 Collected works.

190 Encyclopedias, dictionaries, etc.

195 Directories.

200 Biography.

210 History.

250 GENERAL WORKS.

300 General special.

500 CITY-PLANNING MOVEMENT.

510   Organization.

540   Education of public.

565   Action by community.

580   Special aspects.

700 LEGISLATION.

705   Creative.

760   Regulative.

775   Special countries.

CITY PLANNING

800 METHODS OF TECHNICAL PROCEDURE. PROFESSIONAL PRACTICE.
815 Collection and presentation of data.
840 Design, economic and esthetic. Making of city plans.
850 Presentation of city plans.
860 Direction or supervision of construction and maintenance.
875 Consultation. Coöperation of experts.
880 Competitions.

900 STUDY AND TEACHING.
910 Subject matter.
930 Methods.
960 Special countries.
980 Special schools.

COMPOSITION OF CITY PLANS. PLANNING. REPLANNING.
1200 General. General theory and principles of design.
(1205) Special aspects.
1210 Social aspects.
1215 Hygienic aspects.
1225 Economic aspects.
1235 Esthetic aspects.
1270 Historic aspects.
1290 Other.
1300 Data. (Fundamental conditions, existent and predictable.)
1320 Climate, topography, soil, etc.
1400 Population. Social conditions.
1500 Legal and administrative conditions.
1545 Economic and financial conditions.
1600 Organization and subdivision of city area by dominant function. Districting. Districts.
1625 Administrative districts.
1630 Business districts. Industrial districts.
1675 Residential districts.
1715 Agricultural districts, etc.

20

SUMMARY OUTLINE

CITY PLANNING

Elements of city plans (*continued*).

4500   Open spaces devoted to operation of special municipal services.
4550   Grounds of building groups.
4600   Grounds of single buildings.
4800   Vegetation.
4860   Special forms.
(4870)   Special uses.
4875   Street planting.
4900   Lot planting.
4910   Building decoration.
4930   Planting of open spaces.
5000   Other elements.

5200 Types of city plans.

5210   Types distinguished by climate.
5230   Types distinguished by types of population.
5250   Types distinguished by relation to topography.
5300   Types distinguished by dominant function.
5600   Types distinguished by size of city.
5630   Types distinguished by style of city plan, architectural character of city.

6800 City planning, by special countries and cities arranged geographically.

CITY-PLANNING CLASSIFICATION

If used in connection with Library of Congress Classification, prefix NAC to numbers.

0 BIBLIOGRAPHY.

> General only. Special bibliographies go with the special subjects. Cf. Library of Congress Class Z (Bibliography).

PERIODICALS.

> Subdivided by language. Only general periodicals go here; local with 6800+, City planning by special countries and cities.

(1) (General.)
2 American and English.
4 French.
5 German.
14 Other.

15 YEARBOOKS.

SOCIETIES.

> Proceedings, sets of publications.
> For works on formation of societies, their activities, etc., see 513.

(20) (General.)
21 International.
22 United States.
23 Latin America. South America, Central America, Mexico.
25 British Empire.
28 France and Belgium.
29 Germany, Austria.
31 Hungary, Bohemia.
32 Italy.
33 Scandinavia, Holland.
35 Spain and Portugal.
36 Switzerland.
39 Other.

CITY PLANNING

CONGRESSES. CONFERENCES. CONVENTIONS.
Proceedings, etc.

(40)   (General.)

42   Permanent.
Arranged alphabetically by name of congress.

46   Occasional.
Arranged chronologically.

EXHIBITIONS.
Exhibitions in connection with Congresses go here, but with cross-reference from Congresses. Cf. 546, 940.

(50)   (General.)

52   International.

      Local.

55   United States.

60   Europe.

65   Other.

MUSEUMS.

(70)   (General.)

      Local.

75   United States.

80   Europe.

85   Other.

COLLECTED WORKS. General series.
E. g. Städtebauliche Vorträge.

180   Several authors.

185   Individual authors.

190   ENCYCLOPAEDIAS, DICTIONARIES, glossaries, lists of terms.

195   DIRECTORIES

BIOGRAPHY.

200   Collective.

205   Individual. A–Z.

HISTORY, historical development of city plans, historic forms of city with examples.
Cf. 6800+, which gives opportunity for a purely geographical arrangement. This section 210+ may be used to group material for special purposes.

210   Comprehensive, general.

HISTORY, historical development of city plans, historic forms of city with examples (*continued*).
    European.
212   General.
      By period.
215   Ancient cities.
217   Preclassic.
219   Classic.
225   Mediaeval cities.
230   Modern cities.
235   Oriental.
240   American.
245   Other.

GENERAL WORKS.

250   Comprehensive treatises.
254   Outlines, syllabi, charts, diagrams, etc.
258   Pocket-books, tables, etc.
260   Partial works,
        Treating two or more subdivisions of the general subject.

    Essays, addresses, lectures.
      Cf. 542.
265   Collective.
      Miscellaneous.
270   Single.
      When general; specific go with subject.
(280)   General collections of material in special forms.
      Classify here only material which it is desired to keep together as a collection rather than to distribute by subject.
282   Atlases and general collections of plans.
284   Portfolios and general collections of paintings, drawings, sketches, etc.
286   Albums and general collections of photographs, prints, plates, postcards, etc.
288   General collections of lantern slides.
290   General collections of clippings, excerpts, etc.
292   General collections of manuscripts, notes, etc.
294   General collections of books and pamphlets.
      Chosen as typical; *e. g.* "ten books on city planning for an office library."

CITY PLANNING

CITY-PLANNING MOVEMENT (*continued*).
    ACTION BY COMMUNITY (*continued*).
571   Unofficial employment of experts.
        Cf. 875, 1540.
573   Initiating and securing of legislation.
        Cf. 700+.
    SPECIAL ASPECTS.
580   Village improvement movement.
        Cf. 5605.
582   Garden city movement.
        Cf. 5350.
584   Rural improvement movement.
586   Women in city planning movement.
(600)   (Special places.) See 6800+, City planning by special countries and cities.
        However, if desirable, a shorter geographical table, such as Library of Congress Table I of Class N, may be inserted here.
    LEGISLATION.
        Cf. 573. If a special collection is being made in this field, under each subdivision given here, local legislation might be arranged alphabetically by country or city. See also note under 760+, Regulative legislation
700   General.
    CREATIVE.
705   General.
707   General acts.
        e. g. British Housing and Town Planning &c. Act, 1909.
     Creation or empowering of administrative agents.
        Cf. 1520+.
712   General.
714   City-planning departments, commissions, etc.
        Cf. 1535.
716   Other.
     Creation of public properties, rights, etc.
720   General.
722   Acquisition of land and other privately owned property. Eminent domain.
        Condemnation of land, taking of land, etc.
724   Excess condemnation.
728   Redistribution of land. "Lex Adickes."
735   Creation of easements, rights-of-way, etc.
740   Acquisition of privately-owned utilities.

LEGISLATION (*continued*).

REGULATIVE.

760 General.

(765) (Special.) For regulative legislation relating to special subjects (*e. g.* Districts, Streets, Buildings, Parks) see the special subjects, subhead Legislation. See Index, under Legislation.

SPECIAL COUNTRIES.

Put here, if desirable, collected legislation of special countries or localities.

775 United States.

780 Europe.

785 Other.

METHODS OF TECHNICAL PROCEDURE. PROFESSIONAL PRACTICE.

Cf. subhead Special professional considerations under Elements (*e. g.* Bridges). See Index, under Professional considerations.

800 General.

805 General special.

810 Legislation. Regulation.

COLLECTION AND PRESENTATION OF DATA. MAKING OF SURVEYS.

In general; local works go in 6800+. Cf. Data 1300+. Put here *Methods* of collecting and presenting data, etc. Discussions or general collections of data go in 1300+.

815 General.

Special classes.

820 Topographic, etc.
Cf. 1320+.

822 Social, etc.
Cf. 1400+.

824 Legal and administrative.
Cf. 1500+.

826 Economic and financial.
Cf. 1545+.

Forms of presentation of data.

830 General.

METHODS OF TECHNICAL PROCEDURE. PROFESSIONAL
PRACTICE (*continued*).
COLLECTION AND PRESENTATION OF DATA.
MAKING OF SURVEYS.
Forms of presentation of data (*continued*).

832   Reports, tabulations, compilations, censuses, etc.
Cf. 852.

834   Maps, etc.
Cf. 854.

836   Models.
Cf. 856.

838   Photographs, etc.

DESIGN, economic and esthetic. Making of city plans.
Cf. 914, 1200.

840   General.
842   Studies.
844   Preliminary planning.
846   Revision and amplification.
848   Details.

PRESENTATION OF CITY PLANS.

850   General.
852   Reports.
Cf. 832.

854   Drawings, plans, etc.
Cf. 834.

856   Models.
Cf. 836.

858   Estimates.

860   DIRECTION OR SUPERVISION OF CONSTRUCTION AND MAINTENANCE.
Cf. subhead Construction and maintenance under the individual Elements, (*e. g.* Streets, Parks). See Index.

875   CONSULTATION. COÖPERATION OF EXPERTS.
Cf. 571, 1540.

880   COMPETITIONS.
Material relating to special competitions may be classified by the subject of the competition, or grouped here, according to convenience.

CITY PLANNING

CITY PLANNING

COMPOSITION OF CITY PLANS. PLANNING. REPLAN-
NING.

1200 GENERAL. General theory and principles of
design.

> Cf. 840+, 914, and subhead Design under Elements
> (e. g. Streets, Parks). See Index.

(1205) SPECIAL ASPECTS. General considerations. Broad
relations.

> Cf. 1300+, Data, and subhead Special aspects under
> Elements. See Index.

1210 SOCIAL ASPECTS. Social ethics.

> Cf. 1400+ and subhead Social aspects under Elements
> (e. g. Open spaces). See Index.

1215 HYGIENIC ASPECTS. Public health.

> Cf. 1445+ and subhead Hygienic aspects under Ele-
> ments (e. g. Open spaces). See Index.

1225 ECONOMIC ASPECTS. Efficiency of the community. Municipal government.

> Cf. subhead Economic aspects under Elements (e. g.
> Blocks and lots). See Index.

ESTHETIC ASPECTS. Civic beauty. Civic art.
Municipal art.

> Cf. subhead Esthetic aspects under Elements (e. g.
> Buildings). See Index

1235 General.
1240 General special.
1242 Organic beauty of city.
1244 Birdseye views. Aerial views.

> Including views from eminences.

1246 Influence of aviation on planning for appearance of city.
1248 Silhouette, skyline.
1250 Visual compositions seen from given points.
Views.
1252 Vistas. Termini.
1253 Open.
1254 Closed.
1256 Color.

> Cf. 3517.

1260 City at night. Lighting effects.

> Cf. 1476.

31

CITY PLANNING

CITY PLANNING

CITY PLANNING

COMPOSITION OF CITY PLANS. PLANNING. REPLAN-
NING (*continued*).
DATA. Fundamental conditions.
CLIMATE, TOPOGRAPHY, SOIL, etc.
Topography. City sites.
Land forms (*continued*).

1352	Plains, prairies, marshes. Cf. 5270.
1354	Valleys. Cf. 5280.
1356	Hills, slopes, hilltops. Cf. 4220, 5285, 5290.
	Water bodies, shores, waterfronts. Cf. 2640+, 4170+.
1360	General.
1365	General special.
1367	Use of shores, waterfronts. Cf. 2640+, 4170+.
(1368)	(Reclamation of shores.) See 1347.
1370	Coast, shores. Of sea, arm of sea, or large lake. Cf. 4181, 4182, 5255.
1372	Islands. Cf. 4184, 5260.
1374	Small lakes. Cf. 4182.
1376	Rivers, streams. Cf. 2580+, 4183, 5265.
	Soil. Ground water. Including subsoil. Cf. 1557.
1380	General.
1382	Soil. Geological character. Types of soil. *E. g.* rock, gravel, sand, clay, peat, loam. Cf. 1715, Agricultural districts, and 4800+, Vegetation.
1386	Ground water. Flow of underground water, water-table.
1390	Other natural conditions.
1392	Volcanoes, earthquakes, etc.
	POPULATION. SOCIAL CONDITIONS. Man-made environment. Cf. 822, 5230.
1400	General.

CITY PLANNING

COMPOSITION OF CITY PLANS. PLANNING. REPLAN-
NING (*continued*).
  DATA. Fundamental conditions.
    POPULATION . . . environment.
      Public health and safety.
        Disposal of wastes.
          Water borne (*continued*).

1466   Surface water.
              Cf. 2890.

1470   Non-water-borne.
1472   Garbage, refuse, rubbish, etc.
              Dumps, incinerators, etc. Cf. 4538.

1474   Street cleaning.
1475   Snow removal.
1476   Lighting.
           Cf. 1260, 3870.

1478   Fire protection.
           Cf. 2652, 2888, 3540+, 3568.

1479   Conflagrations. Fires.
           Cf. 1617.

1480   Defence.
           Cf. 2625, 3810+.

1485   Other.
1490   Public education.
        Cf. 3570.

1495   Public recreation.
        Cf. 3575, 3728, 4000+.

1499   Other.

    LEGAL AND ADMINISTRATIVE CONDITIONS.
      Limitations of existing legislation, administrative con-
      ditions, etc. Cf. 824.

1500   General.
      Legal.
        Cf. 700+. But here only Laws as data.

1505   General.
1510   Laws relating to public property, rights, etc.
1515   Laws relating to private property, rights,
        etc.
      Administrative.
        Cf. 712+, where laws relating to creation of ad-
        ministrative agents should go.

COMPOSITION OF CITY PLANS. PLANNING. REPLAN-
NING (*continued*).
DATA. Fundamental conditions.
LEGAL AND ADMINISTRATIVE CONDITIONS.
Administrative (*continued*).

1520   General.
     Public agencies.
1525   General.
1526   General special.
1527   Relation of federal, state, and municipal agencies.
> Cf. 712+, 1590.

1530   Existing.
> City engineers' departments, departments of public works, street departments, water and sewerage boards, park departments, harbor boards and port directors, etc.

1535   Specially created.
> City-planning departments, city-planning commissions, art commissions, etc. Cf. 714.

1540   Public consultation of experts, official employment of experts.
> Cf. 571, 875.

     Private agencies.
1541   Public service corporations.
(1542)   (Societies, etc.) See 500+.

ECONOMIC AND FINANCIAL CONDITIONS. Resources.
> Cf. 826.

1545   General.
     Economic.
1550   General.
1555   Advantages (or disadvantages) of situation
of city.
> Cf. 1340+.

1557   Natural resources.
> Fertile soil, mineral wealth, water-power, etc. Cf. 1380+.

1559   Commercial and industrial opportunities.
1563   Use of land, land values.
> Cf. 4016, and Library of Congress Class HD (section relating to Land).

CITY PLANNING

COMPOSITION OF CITY PLANS. PLANNING. REPLAN-
NING (*continued*).
ORGANIZATION . . . DISTRICTS (*continued*).

1625 ADMINISTRATIVE DISTRICTS.

1627 Civic centers.

> Cf. 3720, (4570). Material may be grouped in 1627 or 3720, according to point of view desired.

BUSINESS DISTRICTS. INDUSTRIAL DISTRICTS.

> Cf. 2640+, 3190+.

1630 General.

1631 General special.

1633 Relation to transportation facilities.

1635 Location, urban *vs.* suburban. Industrial suburbs, "garden city" principle of
location and development, etc.

> Cf. 5350.

1640 Density of development, intensiveness of occupancy, general character of build-
ing development.

> Height, cf. 3480+; materials, cf. 3510+; fireproof-ing, cf. 3540+; etc.

1645 Financial districts.

> Cf. 3600.

1650 Manufacturing districts.

> Cf. 2740, 3195, 3595.

1655 Warehouse, shipping districts.

> Cf. 2718, 3200, 3605.

1660 Market districts.

> Cf. 2827, 3610, 4425.

1665 Wholesale districts.

1670 Retail districts.

> Cf. 3210, 3600.

RESIDENTIAL DISTRICTS.

> Cf. 1430+, 2235+, 3230+, 3380+, 3620+, 5530+.

1675 General.

1676 General special.

1677 Density of development. Intensiveness of
occupancy. Number of houses to
acre.

CITY PLANNING

COMPOSITION OF CITY PLANS. PLANNING. REPLAN-
NING (*continued*).
 ORGANIZATION . . . DISTRICTS.
  RESIDENTIAL DISTRICTS.
   Special types.
    Detached houses (*continued*).

1706	Single.
	Cf. 3651+.
1707	Semi-detached.
	Cf. 3656+.
1708	Other.

AGRICULTURAL DISTRICTS, agricultural belts,
 forest belts.
  Cf. 1380+, (3244).

1715	General.
1720	Agricultural belts.
1723	Market-garden areas.
1724	Allotment gardens.
(1725)	(Forest belts.) See 4160, Forest reservations.

RECREATION AREAS.
 Cf. (3245), 4000+.

1730	General. Distribution.
1731	General special.
1733	Relation to transportation facilities.

BOUNDARY AREAS. Boundaries.
 Cf. 1715+, Agricultural and forest belts.

1745	General.
1748	Approaches and entrances.
	Cf. 2750+, Terminal facilities.
1750	City boundaries.
	Cf. 3815, City walls.

ORGANIZATION AND SUBDIVISION OF CITY AREA INTO
 STREETS AND BLOCKS. Land subdivision,
 in the larger sense.
  Cf. 3000+.

1800	General.
1805	General special.
1810	LOCATION OF MAIN THOROUGHFARES.
	Cf. 2170+.
1812	Determining centers, goals, foci.
1814	Determining connecting routes.

COMPOSITION OF CITY PLANS. PLANNING. REPLANNING (*continued*).

ORGANIZATION . . . STREETS AND BLOCKS (*continued*).

1820   LOCATION OF MINOR STREETS.
Cf. 2220+.

TYPES OF PLATS.
Cf. 5635+.

1830   General.

Formal.
Cf. 5635+.

1835   General.

1837   Gridiron.
Cf. 5637.

1839   Gridiron and diagonal.
Cf. 5639.

1841   Radius and round-point.
Cf. 5641.

1844   Other.

Informal.
Cf. 5645+.

1845   General.

1847   Rectilinear.
Cf. 5647.

1849   Curvilinear.
Cf. 5649.

1851   Composite.
Cf. 5651.

ELEMENTS OF CITY PLANS.
Cf. 916.

1900   General. Collective.

CHANNELS OF TRANSPORTATION. Of persons commodities, power. Ways, conduits, wires.
Cf. 1440, and Library of Congress Class HE (Transportation and communication).

2000   General.

2005   General special.

2010   Special aspects.

2011   Topographic.

2012   Social.

ELEMENTS OF CITY PLANS (*continued*).
CHANNELS OF TRANSPORTATION.
Special aspects (*continued*).

2013	Hygienic.
2014	Economic.
2015	Esthetic.
2016	Historic.
2020	Legislation.
2025	Special professional considerations.
2026	Data.
2027	Design.
2028	Construction and maintenance.
2029	Cost.

STREETS, ROADS. FOOTWAYS.

2050	General.
2055	General special.
2057	Influence of traffic on street-form, street-plan, etc. Congestion of traffic.
2058	Influence on streets of changes in means of transportation. Development of motor traffic.
2060	Special aspects.
2070	Legislation.
	Including street-traffic regulation.
2075	Special professional considerations.
2076	Data.
	Traffic censuses, data on vehicles (*e. g.* motor trucks).
2077	Design.
2078	Construction and maintenance.
2079	Cost.
2085	Form,
	Straight or curved.
2090	Orientation.
	Cf. 3060.
2095	Length, continuity.
2100	Gradient.
2103	Treatment of steep gradients.
	Width. Cross-section.
	Cf. 2356.

CITY PLANNING

ELEMENTS OF CITY PLANS (*continued*).
CHANNELS OF TRANSPORTATION.
STREETS, ROADS. FOOTWAYS.
Width. Cross-section (*continued*).

2105	General.
	Special components.
(2107)	(Separate roadways.) See 2115, Multiple streets.
(2108)	(Walks.) See 2252, Footways.
(2109)	(Planting strips. Parking. Reservations.) See 4875+, Street planting, and 2382, Street-railway reservations.
2110	Special topography. Hillside streets.
2115	Streets specially subdivided. Multiple streets.
2116	Parked streets.
2118	Streets with irrigation canals.
	E. g. as in Boulder, Colo.
2119	Double-deck streets, two-story streets.
	Surface. Pavements.
	Cf. Library of Congress Class TE (Roads and pavements).
2120	General.
2121	Special kinds, arranged alphabetically.
2122	Gutters, curbs.
2124	Drain inlets, man-hole covers, etc.
	Cf. (2306).
2128	Crossings, isles of safety.
	Street junctions.
2135	General.
2136	Intersection of lines of traffic, avoidance of collision points.
2138	Viaducts to avoid crossings at grade.
	Cf. 2513, 3740+.
2150	Proportion of street area to block area.
	Relation to buildings.
2155	General.
2157	Set-backs.
	Cf. 3081.

Elements of city plans (*continued*).
    Channels of transportation.
      Streets, roads. Footways.
        Relation to buildings (*continued*).

2159	Encroachments of buildings, balconies, stoops, marquees, projections, etc.
2161	Arcades, colonnaded streets, covered streetways, galleries.
2163	Relation to height of buildings.

           Cf. 3083, 3480+.

        Thoroughfares. Highways. "Traffic streets."
        Cf. 1810+.

          Including interurban highways.

2170	General.
2175	General special.
2180	Special forms.
2182	Radial.
2183	Circumferential, peripheral. Ringstrassen.
2184	Diagonal.
2188	Other.
	Special uses.
	For business traffic.

           Cf. 4891.

2195	General.
2197	Traffic squares. Roundpoints.

           Cf. (4420).

2199	Cabstands.
2201	One-way streets.
	For pleasure traffic. Drives.

           Cf. (4196), 4893.

2205	General.
2207	Formal. Boulevards, etc.
2209	Informal. Parkways, etc.
2211	Concourses.
2213	Bridle paths.
2214	Bicycle paths.
	Local streets.

        Cf. 1820.

2220	General.

ELEMENTS OF CITY PLANS (*continued*).
  CHANNELS OF TRANSPORTATION.
    STREETS, ROADS. FOOTWAYS.
      Local streets (*continued*).

2225	General special.
	Special uses.
2230	For business. As frontage for business buildings, etc.
	Cf. 1630+, 4891.
2233	Business squares.
	For residence. Residential streets.
	Cf. 1675+, 4892.
2235	General.
2236	Urban.
2237	Suburban.
2238	"Places," residential squares.
	Special forms.
2242	Alleys.
	Cf. 3181.
2244	Private ways.
	Footways.
2250	General.
2252	Sidewalks. Walks.
2254	Independent footways.
2256	Steps, ramps, etc.
2258	Promenades, malls, etc.
	Cf. 4197.
2262	Footbridges and tunnels.
	Cf. 3740+.
	Highway bridges and tunnels.
	Cf. 3740+
2270	General.
2272	Special purposes, to cross water, railroads, highways, etc.
2276	Approaches.
	Cf. 2405.
2278	Draws.
2282	Elevators, lifts, etc.
	Cf. 2526.

CITY PLANNING

ELEMENTS OF CITY PLANS (*continued*).
  CHANNELS OF TRANSPORTATION.
    STREETS, ROADS. FOOTWAYS.
      Highway bridges and tunnels (*continued*).

2284	Subsidiary uses.
2286	Bridges. Culverts.
2288	Tunnels.

Street furniture.
  Cf. 3860.

2290	General.
2292	Street name-plates.

  Cf. (3850).

2294	Poles and wires.

  Cf. 2386.

2296	Police-boxes, fire-alarm boxes. Letter-boxes.
(2298)	(Clocks.) See 3855.
(2302)	(Drinking fountains, troughs.) See 3849.
2304	Hydrants.
(2306)	(Man-hole covers, drain inlets, etc.) See 2124.
(2308)	(Waste cans, etc.) See 3860.
2309	Other.
(2310)	(Street lighting, street-lighting fixtures, lamp-posts, electroliers, etc.) See 3870.
(2315)	(Street planting.) See 4875+.
2320	Street decoration for festivals.

Sub-surface utilities in relation to the street.

2325	General.
2328	Special subways.

  Cf. 2400, Rapid transit subways.

(2329)	(Special utilities, *e. g.* sewerage, telephone.) See 2850+.

STREET-RAILWAYS.   Rapid-transit facilities.
  Including interurban street-railways.   Cf. 1633, 1687, 1733, (2780), 2807.

2350	General.
2355	General special.
2356	Relation to street. Connections between transportation lines at different levels, subway approaches.

  Cf. 2105+.

CITY PLANNING

CITY PLANNING

Elements of city plans (*continued*).
 Channels of transportation.
  Railroads (*continued*).

   Station places.   Station squares.   Station
     grounds.
       Cf. (4423).
2485   General.
2486   Urban.
2487   Suburban.
2488   Village.
2490   Train yards.
2495   Freight houses and yards.
    Rights-of-way.
2500   General.
2502   Through lines.
2504   Belt lines.
2510   Crossings.
2512   At grade.   Grade crossings.
2513   Not at grade.
       Cf. 2138.

   Railroad bridges and tunnels.
       Cf. 3740+.
2515   General.
2516   To cross land.
2517   To cross water.
2520   Special uses.
2522   Freight tunnels.
2524   Draws.
2526   Elevators, lifts.
       Cf. 2282.
2528   Bridges.
2529   Tunnels.

 Waterways and waterfronts, Commercial.
       Cf. (2790), 5317, and Library of Congress Class TC
       (Hydraulic engineering).
2550   General.
2555   General special.
2560   Special aspects.
2570   Legislation.
       Including port regulation.

48

ELEMENTS OF CITY PLANS (*continued*).
    CHANNELS OF TRANSPORTATION.
      WATERWAYS AND WATERFRONTS, COMMERCIAL
        (*continued*).

2575	Special professional considerations.
	Rivers, canals.
	Cf. 1376, 5265.
2580	General.
2585	Channels.
2588	Locks.
(2590)	(Banks.) See 2640+, Waterfronts.
(2595)	(Bridges.) See 3740+, and references from there.
	Bays, harbors, basins.
2600	General.
2605	Channels and anchorages.
	Location, marking, dredging, etc.
2608	Lighthouses.
2610	Harbor lines, bulkhead lines, etc.
	Protective works.
	Cf. 3800.
2615	General.
2617	Breakwaters, jetties, etc.
2619	Sea walls.
2625	Defensive works.
	Cf. 1480, 3810+. 5313.
2630	Harbors and basins for special purposes.
	E. g. fishing fleet, yachting fleet.
	Waterfronts.
	For recreational waterfronts, see 4170+.
2640	General.
2645	General special.
	Special.
2650	Capacity, frontage.
2652	Fire protection.
	Cf. 1478.
	Docks, slips, etc.
2660	General.
2665	Special.
	E. g. size.

CITY PLANNING

ELEMENTS OF CITY PLANS (*continued*).
  CHANNELS OF TRANSPORTATION.
    WATERWAYS AND WATERFRONTS, COMMERCIAL.
    Waterfronts.
      Docks, slips, etc. (*continued*).

2670	Docking apparatus.
2675	Ferry slips.

        Wharves, piers, jetties, quays, etc.

For recreation piers, see 4199.

2680	General.
2685	Special.

E. g. length.

2690	Administration quarters, including quarantine, revenue service, accommodation for employees.

        Special provision for passengers.

Cf. 2800+.

2695	General.
2697	Landing stages.
2699	Shelters, waiting places, etc.
2701	Areas for vehicles.

E. g. cars, cabs, motor vehicles.

        Special provision for freight.

Cf. 2820+.

2710	General.
2712	Freight handling apparatus.
2714	Railroad lines.

Cf. 2450+.

2716	Areas for vehicles.

E. g. drays, motor trucks.

2718	Warehouses, sheds.

Cf. 3605.

2720	Areas for handling and storing special classes of freight.
2722	Grain, grain elevators.
2723	Lumber, coal, stone, gravel, etc. — yards.

Cf. 3197

ELEMENTS OF CITY PLANS (*continued*).
CHANNELS OF TRANSPORTATION.
WATERWAYS AND WATERFRONTS, COMMERCIAL.
Waterfronts.
Wharves, piers, jetties, quays, etc.
Special provision for freight.
Areas for handling . . . freight (*continued*).

2724	Oil, chemicals, explosives.
2725	Perishable goods, cold storage goods.
2729	Other.
2730	Storage areas.

For roofed storage areas, see 2718. For storage areas for special classes of freight, see 2720+.

2735	Shipyards. Drydocks.
2740	Industrial areas, utilization of waterfront by manufacturing plants.

Cf. 1650.

TERMINAL FACILITIES.

2750	General.
2755	General special.
2760	Special aspects.
2770	Legislation.
2775	Special professional considerations.
	Types, by mode of transportation.
(2780)	(Interurban street-railways.) See 2350+.
(2785)	(Railroads.) See 2450+.
(2790)	(Waterways and waterfronts.) See 2550+.
2795	Aerial transportation terminals. Aviation landing places.

Cf. 4384.

Types, by kind of traffic.
Passenger.
Cf. 2695+.

2800	General.
2805	General special.
2807	Relation to local transportation and rapid transit.

Cf. 2350+.

Freight.
Cf. 2522, 2710+.

ELEMENTS OF CITY PLANS (*continued*).
  CHANNELS OF TRANSPORTATION.
    TERMINAL FACILITIES.
      Types, by kind of traffic.
        Freight (*continued*).

2820   General.
2825   General special.
2827   Relation to markets.
                Cf. 1660.
2829   Transshipment.   "Free ports."

CONDUITS. WIRES.

2850   General.
2855   General special.
2857   Relation to street maintenance.
2860   Special aspects.
2870   Legislation.
2875   Special professional considerations.
          Conduits, pipes, etc.
             Culverts, see 2273. Cf. Library of Congress Class TD. (Sanitary and municipal engineering.)
2880   General.
2885   Water-supply and distribution, including aqueducts.
             For monumental aqueducts, see 3740+. Cf. 1456.
2888   Auxiliary high-pressure fire-protection water-supply.
             Cf. 1478.
2890   Sewerage and surface drainage systems.
             Cf. 1452, 1462+.
2895   Subsurface drainage systems.
             Cf. 1452.
2900   Gas distribution.
2905   Pneumatic tubes.
2910   Other.
        Wires.
          Cf. 4856.
2915   General.
2920 ·   General special.
2922   Removal of overhead wires.

ELEMENTS OF CITY PLANS (*continued*).
CHANNELS OF TRANSPORTATION.
CONDUITS. WIRES.
Wires (*continued*).

2925	Power, light, and heat wires.
2930	Telephone and telegraph wires.
2935	"Wireless" apparatus.

BLOCKS * AND LOTS. LAND SUBDIVISION.

In usual sense. Cf. 1800+ and 3380+. Put here general material relating to both blocks and lots, putting special material relating to one alone under Blocks or Lots. The full subdivision is given under each of the three headings to provide for the arrangement of graphic material. For printed material, use principally Blocks and lots, and Lots, putting under Blocks only special material such as would come in 3150–3220.

3000	General.
3005	General special.
3010	Special aspects.
3011	Topographic.
3012	Social.
3013	Hygienic.
3014	Economic.
	Real estate.
3015	Esthetic.
3016	Historic.
3020	Legislation. Restrictions.
	Cf. 1620. Zoning.
3025	Special professional considerations.
3026	Data.
3027	Design.
3028	Construction and maintenance.
3029	Cost.
	Size, shape, orientation, topography. Adaptability to development.
	Cf. 3120+, 3270+.
3040	General.
3045	Size. Dimensions.
	Cf. 3125, 3275.

* Block is used in the sense of an area of ground, not in its popular sense, houses in-block.

CITY PLANNING

CITY PLANNING

ELEMENTS OF CITY PLANS (continued).
BLOCKS AND LOTS. LAND SUBDIVISION.
Size, shape . . . Adaptability to development
(continued).

Shape. Proportions.
Cf. 3050, 3280+.

3130	General.
3131	Rectangular.

Cf. 3282.

3133	Tapering.
3135	With one side or more curvilinear.
3139	Other.
3140	Orientation.

Cf. 3060, 3290.

3145	Topography.

Cf. 3065, 3293+.

3150	Relation to other blocks.
3151	Equality.
3152	Dominance or subordination.
3155	Relation to street.

Cf. 3070, 3305+.

3160	Subdivision into lots.
3163	Fluctuation in sizes of component lots.

Relation of area to buildings thereon.
Cf. 3075+, 3315+.

3165	General.
3167	Proportion of built-over area.
3169	Disposition of built-over area.
3177	Disposition of unbuilt-over area.

Cf. 3087+, 3327.

3179	Courts, block interiors.

Cf. 3089.

3181	Passageways, alleys, etc. Access to interiors.

Cf. 2242, 3091.

3183	Corner reservations.

Cf. 3308.

55

ELEMENTS OF CITY PLANS (*continued*).
    BLOCKS AND LOTS. LAND SUBDIVISION.
      BLOCKS (*continued*).

        Special types of occupancy.
        Business.
            Cf. 1630+.

3190	General.
3195	Manufacturing plants.
	Buildings and grounds. Cf. 3595.
3197	Brick-yards, lumber-yards, tan-yards, stock-yards, etc.
	Cf. 2725.
3199	Pleasure grounds for employees.
3200	Warehouses.
	Cf. 1655, 3605.
3205	Office buildings.
	Cf. 3600.
3210	Retail shops.
	Cf. 1670, 3600.
3220	Other.

        Residence.
            Cf. 1675+, 3380+, 3620+.

3230	General.
3235	Houses in-block.
	Cf. 1700+, 3635+.
3240	Detached houses.
	Cf. 1705+, 3650+.
(3244)	(Agriculture.) See **1715+**.
(3245)	(Open-air recreation.) See 4000.

     LOTS.
       See note under 3000+. Blocks and lots.

3250	General.
3255	General special.
3265	Special professional considerations.
3269	Cost.

       Size, shape, orientation, topography. Adaptability to development.
          Cf. 3040+, 3120+.

3270	General.

ELEMENTS OF CITY PLANS (*continued*).
  BLOCKS AND LOTS. LAND SUBDIVISION.
    LOTS.
      Relation of area to buildings . . . (*continued*).

3327	Disposition of unbuilt-over area.
	Cf. 3087 + 3177.
3329	Gardens.
(3330)	(Dooryard). See 4901.
(3331)	(Backyard.) See 4902.
3334	Other.

      Special types of occupancy.

(3340)	(Business.) See 3190 +, Blocks.
	Residential. Land subdivision for residences.
	Cf. 1675 +, 3230 +, 3620 +.
3380	General.
3385	Large estates.
3390	Suburban places.
3395	Building lots. House lots.

  STRUCTURES. Architectural and engineering, except structures constituting channels of transportation.
    For these see 2000 +.

3400	General.
3405	General special.
3410	Special aspects.
3415	Esthetic.
3416	Historic.
3419	Other.
(3420)	(Legislation.)
3425	Special professional considerations.

  BUILDINGS.
    Cf. Library of Congress Class NA (Architecture) and TH (Building construction).

3440	General.
3445	General special.
3448	Relation to surroundings.
	Cf. 4550 +, 4600 +.
3450	Special aspects.
3452	Social.

Elements of city plans (*continued*).
  Structures.
    Buildings.
      Special aspects (*continued*).
3453   Hygienic.
3455   Esthetic.
                General effect of style, scale, etc. Consistency.
3456   Historic.
3460   Legislation.
                Including building laws, building codes, restrictions
                affecting appearance, etc. Cf. 1620, Zoning; 3081.
                Building lines; 3083, Building heights.

3465   Special professional considerations.
3466   Data.
3467   Design.
3468   Construction and maintenance.
3469   Cost.
      Form.
3475   General.
3480   Size. Height.
                Cf. 1640, 2163, 3083, 5660.

3489   "Skyscrapers."
                Cf. 5660.

3490   Style.
                Architectural. Cf. 5690.

3500   Special elements.
3502   Domes, spires, towers, etc.
3504   Roofs, etc.
3506   Walls, doors, windows, etc.
3509   Other.

      Materials.
                Cf. 1640, 5680.

3510   General.
3515   General special.
3517   Color.   .
                Cf. 1256.

3520   Structural materials.
3521   Wood.
3523   Brick and tile.

59

ELEMENTS OF CITY PLANS (*continued*).
  STRUCTURES.
    BUILDINGS.
      Materials.
        Structural materials (*continued.*)

3524	Stone.
3526	Concrete.
3527	Reinforced concrete.
3528	Iron and steel.
3529	Other.

            Special surface treatment.

3535	Stucco-plaster.
3539	Other.

        Types of construction.*

> Cf. 1478, and Library of Congress, Class TH (Building construction).

3540   General.

3542   Fire-resistive.

> Masonry walls, incombustible floors.

3543   Semi-fire-resistive.

> Masonry walls, wooden floors.

3544   Combustible.

> Wooden walls and floors.

3549   Other.

        Buildings for special uses.

> Cf. 4600+. Probably better to concentrate material here in 3560+ unless there is a special reason for doing otherwise. If it is desired to subdivide under each group, buildings may be arranged alphabetically by kind of building.

3560   General.   Collective.

3563   Public buildings.

> Including federal, state, and municipal buildings.

3565   Administration.

> Including capitols, city halls, court houses, etc.

3568   Special municipal services.

> Including pumping stations, water-towers, standpipes, power houses, gas tanks, fire stations, police stations, prisons, etc. Cf. 4500+, Open spaces devoted to operation of special municipal services.

* Classification by Professor C. W. Killam, Harvard University.

Elements of city plans (*continued*).
STRUCTURES.
BUILDINGS.
Buildings for special uses (*continued*).

3570	Educational buildings.
	Schools, libraries, museums, etc. Cf. 3722.
3575	Buildings for recreation.
	Opera houses, theatres, auditoriums, etc. Cf. 3728.
3580	Public baths, gymnasia, etc.
3585	Hospitals, asylums, etc.
3590	Churches.
3595	Buildings for manufacturing.
	Factories, mills, etc. Cf. 3195.
3600	Buildings for business and commerce.
	Shops, office buildings, banks, etc. Cf. 3205, 3210.
3605	Buildings for transportation and storage.
	Railroad stations, Cf. 2480; Warehouses, Cf. 1655, 2718, 3200, etc.
3610	Markets.
	Cf. 1660.
3618	Hotels, clubs, etc.
	Residences.
	Cf. 1430+, 1675+, 3230+, 3380+.
3620	General.
3625	General special.
(3630)	Special types.
	Houses in-block.
	Cf. 1700+, 3235.
3635	General.
3636	Single.
	Cf. 1701.
3637	High-cost.
	Cf. 1695.
3638	Medium-cost.
	Cf. 1696.
3639	Low-cost.
	Cf. 1697.
3641	Multiple.
3642	High-cost. High class apartments.
	Cf. 1695, 1702.

ELEMENTS OF CITY PLANS (*continued*).
STRUCTURES.
BUILDINGS.
Buildings for special uses.
Residences.
Special types.
Houses in-block.
Multiple (*continued*).

3643   Medium-cost.
Cf. 1696.

3644   Low-cost. Tenements.
Cf. 1697, 1703.

Detached houses.
Cf. 1705+, 3240.

3650   General.
3651   Single.
Cf. 1706.

3652   High-cost.
Cf. 1695.

3653   Medium-cost.
Cf. 1696.

3654   Low-cost. Cottages.
Cf. 1697.

3656   Semi-detached.
Cf. 1707.

3658   Medium-cost.
Cf. 1696.

3659   Low-cost.
Cf. 1697.

3669   Other.
Minor buildings.
3670   General.
3675   Shelters, pavilions.
Cf. 2410, 4137, 4345.

3677   Public comfort stations.
3681   Bandstands, etc.
3684   Booths, street-stands.
3687   Greenhouses.
Cf. 4545.

3689   Other.

CITY PLANNING

ELEMENTS OF CITY PLANS (*continued*).
   STRUCTURES.
      BUILDINGS (*continued*).
         Building groups.

> Cf. 4550+. Probably better to concentrate material here in 3700+ as under Buildings, unless there is a special reason for doing otherwise.

3700	General.
3705	General special.
3710	Design.

> Of groups as wholes. Interrelation of buildings in groups. For design of buildings individually, see 3440+.

(3715)	Building groups for special uses.

> This section may be expanded to correspond with 3560+.

3720	Administrative, etc.

> Cf. 1627, 3565, (4570).

3722	Educational, etc.

> Cf. 3570.

3724	Exposition groups.

> Cf. (4585).

3728	Recreational, etc.

> Cf. 3575.

3739	Other.

      BRIDGES. VIADUCTS.

> Including monumental aqueducts. Cf. 2138, 2390. 2885, and Library of Congress Class TG (Bridges, etc.). Put here general material on bridges and viaducts considered as structures, *e. g.* bridge design — architectural and engineering considerations. For special treatises on Bridges in connection with transportation, see note under 3790.

3740	General.
3745	General special.
3750	Special aspects.
3760	Legislation.
3765	Special professional considerations.
3770	Form.
3780	Materials.
(3790)	(Bridges and viaducts for special uses.) See the special uses: 2270+, Highway bridges; 2262, Footbridges; 2390, Street-railway bridges; 2515+, Railroad bridges.

Elements of city plans (*continued*).
Structures (*continued*).

3800   Dams. Dikes. Levees.
Cf. 1454, 2615+.

Defensive works.
Cf. 1480, 2625, 5311.

3810   General.
3812   Fortifications. Forts.
3815   City walls. City gates.
Cf. 1745+.

Minor structures.
Cf. 3670+, Minor buildings.

3820   General.
3825   Walls, fences, gates, etc. Boundary structures.
Cf. 3304.

3830   Monuments, monumental arches, obelisks, etc.
3840   Statues, including monumental statues.
3845   Fountains, basins, etc.
3849   Drinking fountains, troughs.
Cf. (2302).

(3850)   (Street name-plates.) See 2292.
3855   Clocks.
Cf. (2298).

3857   Flagpoles, flagstaffs.
3860   Street and park furniture.
Seats, waste cans, etc. Cf. 2290+, Street furniture, and 4141, Park furniture. Material may be
grouped according to point of view.

3870   Lighting-fixtures, lamp-posts, electroliers, etc.
Cf. 1476, (2310).

3872   City scales.
3875   Illuminated signs, etc.
3878   Kiosks. Advertising kiosks.
3880   Billboards. Posters. Billboard nuisance.
3882   Shop signs. Commercial street signs.
3885   Other.

ELEMENTS OF CITY PLANS (*continued*).
   STRUCTURES (*continued*).

3890	OTHER.

OPEN SPACES, public and quasi-public, other than for traffic.
       Cf. 1495, 1730, 4930.

4000	General.
4005	General special.
4010	Special aspects.
4011	Topographic.
4012	Social.
4013	Hygienic.
4014	Economic.
4015	Open spaces as obstructions to traffic.
4016	Effect of open spaces on land values.
	Cf. 1563+.
4020	Esthetic.
4021	Preservation of natural landscape.
	Cf. 4225.
4022	Types of treatment, formal and informal.
4025	Historic.
4030	Legislation.
4035	Special professional considerations.

PARK SYSTEMS.
      Put here only material on park systems as such. For the components of park systems, see 4100+, Parks and reservations; 2209, Parkways; 4300+, Playgrounds.

4040	General.
4055	Special professional considerations.
4060	Park systems for special types of cities.
	Cf. subdivisions of 5200+.
4085	Industrial cities.

PARKS AND RESERVATIONS.
      Cf. 4935.

4100	General.
4105	General special.
4106	Encroachments on public parks, buildings in parks.

CITY PLANNING

ELEMENTS OF CITY PLANS (*continued*).
OPEN SPACES . . . other than for traffic.
PARKS AND RESERVATIONS.
General special (*continued*).

4108	Private concessions.
4120	Legislation.

Including park regulation.

4125	Special professional considerations.
4126	Data.
4127	Design.
4128	Construction and maintenance.
4129	Cost.

Provision for comfort and pleasure.

4135	General.
4137	Resting places, shelters, etc.

Cf. 3675.

4139	Outdoor eating places, refreshment places.
4141	Park furniture.

Cf. 3860.

Reservations.

4150	General.
4155	General special.
4160	Forest reservations.

Cf. (1725).

Shore reservations. Recreational water fronts.
Cf. 2640+, Commercial waterfronts.

4170	General.
4175	General special.
4177	Combination with commercial utilization.
4179	Misuse, defacement of shores.

Special situations.

4181	Seashore. Marine parks.

Cf. 1370.

4182	Lake.

Cf. 1370, 1374.

4183	River.

Cf. 1376.

66

Elements of city plans (*continued*).
  Open spaces . . . other than for traffic.
    Parks and reservations.
      Reservations.
        Shore reservations. Recreational water-fronts.
          Special situations (*continued*).

4184	Island.
	Cf. 1372.
4190	Types of treatment, formal and informal.
(4195)	Provision for special forms of recreation.
(4196)	(Drives, shore boulevards.) See 2205 +.
4197	Promenades, embankments.
	Cf. 2258.
4199	Recreation piers.
4201	Bathing beaches.
4203	Boating facilities.
4205	Winter-sport facilities.
4210	Reservoir reservations, not primarily parks.
	Cf. 4510.
4220	Summit reservations, outlooks, etc.
	Cf. 1356.
4225	Places containing special natural features.
	Cf. 4021.
4230	Places of special historic interest.
	Cf. 1276.
4240	Large parks. Country parks.
	Small parks, commons, garden squares, neighborhood parks.
	Cf. (4450).
4250	General.
4255	.Types of treatment.
	Public gardens, etc.
	Cf. 4940.
4260	General.
4265	Botanical gardens.
4270	Zoölogical parks.
4274	Other.
4275	Open-air theatres. Settings for pageants.

ELEMENTS OF CITY PLANS (*continued*).
OPEN SPACES . . . other than for traffic.
PARKS AND RESERVATIONS (*continued*).

4280	Open-air concert and beer "gardens."
4290	Amusement parks. Street-railway parks.

PLAYGROUNDS, ATHLETIC FIELDS. Provision for special sports.

Cf. Library of Congress, Class GV (Sports and amusements).

4300	General.
	Playgrounds.
4310	General.
4315	General special.
4316	Distribution of playgrounds.
4318	As social centers.
4330	Legislation.
4335	Special professional considerations.
4336	Data.
4337	Design.
4338	Construction and maintenance.
4339	Cost.
4345	Shelter buildings.

Cf. 3675.

4350	Swimming pools, wading pools.
4355	Apparatus.
(4360)	(Planting.) See 4945
4370	Athletic fields, ball grounds, etc.
4375	Stadiums.
4380	Race-tracks. Speedways.

Cf. 2209, Parkways.

4384	Aviation grounds. Aerodromes.

Cf. 2795.

4385	Provision for other special sports.
4395	DRILL GROUNDS.

SQUARES.

The subheads enclosed in curves are given to complete the classification of squares. Unless for special purposes, it is not intended that material shall be classified here under those subheads, but rather in the places referred to.

4400	General.

ELEMENTS OF CITY PLANS (*continued*).
OPEN SPACES . . . other than for traffic.
SQUARES (*continued*).

4405	General special.
4415	Special professional considerations.
(4420)	(Traffic.) See 2197.
(4423)	(Station places. Station squares.) See 2485+
4425	Market places. Market squares.

Cf. 1660.

4430	Congregating places, fora, exchange places.
4435	Architectural, Monumental.

Cf. (4575).

(4440)	(Business.) See 2233.
(4445)	(Residential.) See 2238.
(4450)	(Garden.) See 4250+.

CEMETERIES.

For Churchyards and Graveyards, see 4650, Grounds of churches.

4480	General.
4485	General special.
4495	Special professional considerations.

OPEN SPACES DEVOTED TO OPERATION OF SPECIAL MUNICIPAL SERVICES.

Location and design, including location of buildings in area. For construction, engineering features, see Library of Congress, Class TD, (Municipal engineering). For Buildings, see 3568.

4500	General.
4501	General special.
4505	Special professional considerations.
4510	Water-supply areas.

Including reservoirs, basins, filtration plants. Cf. 1456, 4210.

4520	Sewage disposal areas.

Including sewerage plants, sewage disposal plants, sewage farms, filtration beds. Cf. 1464.

4538	Municipal dumps.

Cf. 1472.

4540	Yards, stables, for use of municipal departments. "City yards." Areas for storage of municipal equipment.

E. g. equipment for street cleaning, garbage and rubbish removal.

CITY PLANNING

Elements of city plans (*continued*).

Open spaces devoted to operation of special
MUNICIPAL SERVICES (*continued*).

4545   Municipal nurseries.   Greenhouses.

Cf. 3687.

4549   Other.

Grounds of Building Groups.

Cf. 3700+. This section need not be used unless desirable for special reasons, but all material grouped in
3700+.

4550   General.
4555   General special.
4565   Special professional considerations.

Special types.

(4570)   (Civic centers.)   See 1627, 3720.
(4575)   (Architectural and monumental squares.)
See 4435.
(4585)   (Exposition grounds.)   See 3724.

Grounds of Single Buildings.

Cf. 3560+. This section need not be used unless desirable for special reasons, but all material grouped in
3560+.

4600   General.
4605   General special.
4615   Special professional considerations.
4620   Special types.

Cf. 3560, Buildings for special uses. Same subdivisions can be used here, with same intervals of numbers: *e. g.*, Churchyards, Graveyards, 4650.

Vegetation.

Cf. 1715+, 4160, 4545, and Library of Congress Class SB
(Horticulture, etc.) and SD (Forestry).

4800   General.
4805   General special.
4810   Special aspects.
4811   Climatic.
4813   Hygienic.
4814   Economic.
4815   Esthetic.
4820   Legislation.

ELEMENTS OF CITY PLANS (*continued*).
  VEGETATION (*continued*).
    Special professional considerations.

4825   General.

4830   Data. Choice of vegetation.
          Vegetation adapted to urban conditions, to particular purposes.

4835   Design. Planting design.
      Construction and maintenance.

4840   General.

4842   Cost.

4844   Soil preparation and cultivation. Irrigation.
          Drainage.
          Cf. 1380+.

4846   Protection. Tree guards, railings, etc.
      Prevention and mitigation of adverse conditions.

4850   General.

4852   Insect pests, spraying, etc.

4854   Smoke.
          Cf. 1449.

4856   Wires.
          Cf. 2915.

4858   Underground gas-leaks.

    SPECIAL FORMS.

4860   Trees.
          Cf. 4885.

4861   Shrubs.
          Cf. 4886.

4862   Herbaceous plants.
          Cf. 4887.

4863   Turf.
          Cf. 4888.

(4870)   SPECIAL USES.

    STREET PLANTING.
          Including roadside improvement. Cf. (2109), (2315).

4875   General.

CITY PLANNING

ELEMENTS OF CITY PLANS (*continued*).
  VEGETATION.
    SPECIAL USES.
      STREET PLANTING (*continued*).

4880	General special.
4882	Selection of trees, etc., in regard to width of streets.
	Special forms.
4885	Trees.
	Cf. 4860.
4886	Shrubs.
	Cf. 4861.
4887	Flower beds.
	Cf. 4862.
4888	Turf strips.
	Cf. (2109), 4863.
	Special uses.
4891	Business streets.
	Cf. 2195+.
4892	Residential streets.
	Cf. 2235+.
4893	Parkways, boulevards.
	Cf. 2207, 2209.

      LOT PLANTING.

4900	General.
4901	Dooryard gardens.
	Cf. (3330).
4902	Backyard gardens.
	Cf. (3331).
4905	Vacant lot gardens.
4907	School gardens.
4909	Other.

      BUILDING DECORATION.

4910	General.
4912	Vines.
4914	Window gardens, window boxes, balcony gardens.
4916	Plants (*e. g.* bay trees) in tubs, boxes, pots:
4919	Roof gardens.

CITY PLANNING

ELEMENTS OF CITY PLANS (*continued*).
 VEGETATION.
  SPECIAL USES (*continued*).

   PLANTING OF OPEN SPACES, public and quasi-public, other than for traffic.
    Cf. 4000+.

4930   General.
4935   Parks.
     Cf. 4100+.

4940   Public gardens.
     Cf. 4260+.

4945   Playgrounds.
     Cf. (4360).

5000   OTHER ELEMENTS.

 TYPES OF CITY PLANS.
   General only, or collections of works on individual cities illustrating types; other works on individual cities go with 6800+, City planning, by special countries and cities arranged geographically.

5200   General.
5205   General special.

   TYPES DISTINGUISHED BY CLIMATE.
     Cf. 1330+.

5210   General.
5215   Temperate.
5220   Hot.
5225   Cold.

5230   TYPES DISTINGUISHED BY TYPES OF POPULATION, races, nationalities.
     Cf. 1400+.

   TYPES DISTINGUISHED BY RELATION TO TOPOGRAPHY.
     Cf. 1340+.

5250   General.
5255   Coast or shore cities.
     Cf. 1370.

5260   Island cities.
     Cf. 1372.

Types of city plans (*continued*).

Types distinguished by dominant function (*continued*).

5350   Garden cities. Garden suburbs. Garden villages.

> Cf. 582, 1635, 1685. For convenience all Garden City literature may be collected here with geographical arrangement (use same relation of numbers as given in geographical table); or local material may be put with 6800+, City planning, by special countries and cities.

5550   Other.

5552   Utopias, etc.

Types distinguished by size of city.

5600   General.

5605   Villages,

> To 5000 inhabitants. Cf. 580. Village improvement literature may be collected here.

5610   Small cities.

> 5000–50,000.

5615   Medium-sized cities.

> 50,000–100,000.

5620   Large cities.

> 100,000 to one million.

5625   Largest cities.

> One million and over.

Types distinguished by style of city plan.

Architectural character of city.

5630   General.

Dominant types of plat.

> Cf. 1800+. This section 5635+ is provided particularly to classify graphic material.

Formal.

> Cf. 1835+.

5635   General.

5637   Gridiron.

> Cf. 1837.

5639   Gridiron and diagonal.

> Cf. 1839.

5641   Radius and round-point.

> Cf. 1841.

5644   Other.

Types of City Plans (*continued*).

Types distinguished by style of city plan. . . .
Dominant types of plat (*continued*).
Informal.
Cf. 1845+.

5645	General.
5647	Rectilinear.
	Cf. 1847.
5649	Curvilinear.
	Cf. 1849.
5651	Composite.
	Cf. 1851.
5660	Dominant height of construction. Skyscraper cities.
	Cf. 3480+.
5680	Dominant building materials.
	Brick, wood, etc. Cf. 3510+, 3540+.
5690	Dominant architectural style.
	Cf. 3490.
6800	City planning, by special countries and cities
6984	arranged geographically. See Geographical table, and Subarrangement of material under individual countries and cities, following.

GEOGRAPHICAL TABLE.

This table is substantially that given at the end of Class N, of the Library of Congress Classification, there designated as Table II. It is here numbered ready to use in connection with this City Planning Scheme. It will be noted that the gap left after the number assigned to a country (*e. g.* Canada, 6829, Mexico, 6831) can be used for a separate number assigned to works on individual cities of that country if the user so desires. In that case, for example, works on City Planning in Canada would be numbered 6829, while a work on the Plan of Calgary would be numbered 6830 Cal, (*Cal* being the abbreviation formed from the first few letters of the city name). The School of Landscape Architecture uses this method, which for a very small collection might not be worth while.

It was considered best to publish a full geographical table, especially to provide for the arrangement of descriptive material, photographs, and postcards which might be assembled as data from all over the world.

COUNTRY SUBDIVISIONS.

6801   America.

6803   North America.

6805   United States.

By sections.

To be used only if desired. See note under 6827, Cities.

6810   New England.

6811   South.

6814   Central.

6817   West.

6819   Pacific States.

6825   States A–Z.

6827   Cities A–Z.

It is most convenient to arrange material alphabetically by cities as far as possible.

6829   Canada.

6831   Mexico.

6833   Central America.

6835   British Honduras.

6837   Costa Rica.

6839   Guatemala.

6841   Honduras.

6843   Nicaragua.

6845   Salvador

6846 Panama.
6847 West Indies.
6849   Bahamas.
6851   Cuba.
6853   Haiti.
6855   Jamaica.
6857   Porto Rico.
6858   Other.
6859 South America.
6861   Argentine Republic.
6863   Bolivia.
6865   Brazil.
6867   Chile.
6869   Colombia.
6871   Ecuador.
6873   Guiana.
6875   Paraguay.
6877   Peru.
6879   Uruguay.
6881   Venezuela.
6883 Europe.
6885   Great Britain. England.
6887   England. Local.
6889   Scotland.
6891   Ireland.
6893   Wales.
6895   Austria-Hungary.
6897   France.
6899   Germany.
6901   Greece.
6903   Italy.
6905   Netherlands.
6907   Holland.
6909   Belgium. Flanders.
6911   Russia.
6913   Scandinavia.
6915   Denmark.
6917   Iceland.
6919   Norway.
6921   Sweden.

Europe (*continued*).

6923	Spain. Spain and Portugal.
6925	Portugal.
6927	Switzerland.
6929	Turkey.
6931	Other Balkan States.
6933	Bulgaria.
6935	Montenegro.
6937	Rumania.
6939	Servia.
6941	Others.
6943	Asia. The Orient.
6945	Southwestern Asia. Near East. Levant. Asia Minor. Turkey in Asia.
6947	Persia.
6949	Central Asia.
6951	Southern Asia. India. Ceylon.
6953	Indo-China.
6955	French Indo-China.
6957	Indonesia. Malaysia.
6959	Dutch East Indies.
6961	Philippines.
6963	Eastern Asia.
6965	China.
6967	Japan.
6969	Northern Asia. Siberia. Russia in Asia.
6973	Africa.
6975	North.
6977	South.
6979	Australia.
6981	New Zealand.
6983	Pacific Islands.
6984	Special A–Z.

SUBARRANGEMENT OF MATERIAL UNDER INDIVIDUAL COUNTRIES AND CITIES.

It will very often be necessary to subdivide the material accumulated for individual cities. The simplest method of doing this is to use the number for the city followed by the numbers for the topics as given in the general classification scheme. For example, a man living in Chicago has besides the general city-plan reports for Chicago a large collection of clippings and excerpts relating to Chicago. The designation of Chicago in his files is 6827 Chi (see explanation at beginning of geographical table). His reports, which he arranges chronologically, are numbered 6827 Chi 1909, 6827 Chi 1911, 6827 Chi 1912. By taking the letter A to follow 6827 Chi he can designate that detailed material is to be kept separate from the general chronological arrangement. He then looks over the Summary Outline of the Classification, noting the numbers of the topics on which he has material, and proceeds to designate his clippings as follows, *e. g.* those on Business districts, $\dfrac{6827 \text{ Chi}}{\text{A } 1630}$; those on Streets, $\dfrac{6827 \text{ Chi}}{\text{A } 2050}$; those on Playgrounds, $\dfrac{6827 \text{ Chi}}{\text{A } 4300}$; and so on. The alternative method to the one just described would be to boil down and renumber with letters or small numbers the Summary Outline and then to use these designations in the way just described. This could be done by each individual, especially if he wishes to have only a small number of subdivisions.

Although the numbers resulting from the first method are somewhat long, this disadvantage is far outweighed by the following advantages: a man has only one outline to remember, and only one set of numbers; since the subdivisional numbers under an individual city are the same as the numbers on the general subject, there is an automatic cross-reference both ways — a person wanting everything on playgrounds knows he must look under 4300 both in the general arrangement and under such cities as have been subdivided, while a person studying Boston's playgrounds (6827 Bost A 4300), and wishing to compare these data with general data, can look instantly in 4300; furthermore, material which might appear on any minute topic relating to a given city can be cared for immediately by specific number taken from the fuller scheme.

In case it is desirable to separate material relating to sections of a city from that relating to the city as a whole, this might be placed last and perhaps designated B, so that after general reports and material on special subjects designated e. g. 6827 Bost 1912, $\frac{6827 \text{ Bost}}{\text{A } 4300}$, there would be e. g. $\frac{6827 \text{ Bost}}{\text{B. Rox}}$, for the Roxbury section of Boston.

The above suggestions serve to indicate the possible treatment of a large bulk of local material. The particular purpose for which the material is to be used will of course determine the amount and character of subdivision that will be worth while.

ALPHABETIC SUBJECT INDEX TO CLASSIFICATION

References are to numbers of topics in the Scheme

INDEX

INDEX

Buildings, 3440–3689.
  Form, 3475–3509.
  Grounds, 4600–4620.
  Height, 3083, 3480–3489.
    (Business districts), 1640.
    Relation to street, 2163.
    Types of city plans distinguished by, 5660.
  In parks (Encroachments), 4106.
  Materials, *see* Building materials.
  Relation to
    Block and lot area, 3075–3091.
    Block area, 3165–3183.
    Lot area, 3315–3334.
    Streets, 2155–2163.
  Size, 3480–3489.
  Surface treatment, 3535–3539.
Buildings, Historic, 3456.
Buildings, Shelter, *see* Shelters.
Bulkhead lines, 2610.
Burned districts, Replanning, 1617.
Business blocks, 3190–3220.
Business buildings, 3600.
  Streets as frontage for, 2230.
Business districts, 1630–1670.
Business encroachment on residential districts, 1682.
(Business lots), (3340).
Business squares, 2233.
Business local streets, 2230–2233.
Business streets (In general).
  Planting, 4891.
Business traffic streets, 2195–2201.

C

Cables, Underground, 2386.
Cabstands, 2199.
Campaigns, City-planning, 525.
Canals, 2580–(2595).
Canals, Irrigation, Streets with, 2118
Capitols, 3565.
Car-barns, 2420.
Cemeteries, 4480–4495.
Censuses (Data), 832.
Centers, Determining location of main thoroughfares, 1812.
Centers, Civic, *see* Civic centers.
Chambers of commerce, 515.
Change in type of occupancy, Effects of, 1613.

Channels
  (Commercial rivers), 2585.
  (Harbors), 2605–2608.
Channels of transportation, 2000–2930.
Charts, General, 254.
Chemicals, Areas for handling and storing (Waterfronts), 2724.
Churches, 3590.
Churchyards, 4650.
Circulation (Data), 1440.
Circumferential thoroughfares, 2183.
Cities.
  Large (Types of plans), 5620.
  Largest (Types of plans), 5625.
  Medium-sized (Types of plans), 5615.
  Small (Types of plans), 5610.
  Special (Arranged geographically), 6800–6984.
City.
  Area.
    Organization and subdivision by dominant function, 1600–1740.
    Organization and subdivision into streets and blocks, 1800–1851.
  At night. Lighting effects, 1260.
  Boundaries, 1750.
  Historic forms, 210–245.
  History (Data), 1415.
  Organic beauty, 1242.
  Sites, 1340–1376.
    Economic advantages (Data), 1555–1559.
  See also phrases beginning with words City and Municipal.
City and country, 1422–1426.
City clubs, 517.
City engineers' departments, 1530.
City forestry, *see* Vegetation.
City gates, 3815.
City halls, 3565.
City plan, *see* City plans.
City planning.
  As an art, science, or profession, 320–324.
  By special countries and cities arranged geographically, 6800–6984.
  Field, scope, 310.
  Purpose, utility, 305.

INDEX

89

INDEX

INDEX

Health resorts (Types of plans), 5333.
Heat, light, and power wires, 2925.
Hedges (Lot boundary), 3304.
Height of buildings, see Buildings, Height.
Herbaceous plants, 4862.
High-cost multiple houses in-block, 3642.
High-cost residential districts, 1695.
High-cost single detached houses, 3652.
High-cost single houses in-block, 3637.
High-pressure auxiliary fire-protection water-supply systems, 2888.
Highway bridges, 2270–2284.
Highways, 2170–2211.
Hillside lots, 3295.
Hillside streets, 2110.
Hills, (Topographical data), 1356.
  Removal, 1347.
Hilltop cities (Types of plans), 5290.
Hilltops (Topographical data), 1356.
Historic aspects.
  Blocks and lots, 3016.
  Buildings, 3456.
  Channels of transportation, 2016.
  General, 1270–1276.
  Open spaces, 4025. .
  Structures, 3416.
Historic features in cities, Preservation, 1276.
Historic interest, Places of, Reservation, 4230.
Historic type, Truth of city plans to, 1272.
History of city planning, 210–245.
History of the city (Data), 1415.
Hospitals, 3585.
Hot climate, Types of city plans distinguished by, 5220.
Hotels, 3618.
House lots, 3395.
Houses, Number to acre, 1677.
Houses, Detached, 3650–3669.
  Blocks occupied by, 3240.
  Districts with, 1705–1708.
Houses in-block, 3635–3644.
  Blocks occupied by, 3235.
  Districts with, 1700–1703.
Housing, 1430.
Hydrants, 2304.

Hygienic aspects.
  Blocks and lots, 3013.
  Buildings, 3453.
  Channels of transportation, 2013.
  General, 1215.
  Open spaces, 4013.
  Vegetation, 4813.

I

Illuminated signs, 3875
Improvement, Civic, Rural, etc., see Civic improvement, Rural improvement, etc.
Improvement of conditions, (City-planning movement), 565.
Improvements, Effect on land values, 1567.
Incinerators (Disposal of wastes), 1472.
Income (Municipal finances), 1575–1594.
Individuality (of cities), Preservation, 1274.
Industrial areas (Water-fronts), 2740.
Industrial cities (Types of plans), 5320–5324.
  Park systems for, 4085.
Industrial conditions (Data), 1435.
Industrial districts. Business districts, 1630–1670.
Industrial opportunities (Data), 1559.
Industrial suburbs, 1635.
Informal types of plates, 1845–1851.
  (Types of city plans), 5645–5651.
Insect pests, 4852.
Instruction, see Study and teaching.
Intersection of lines of traffic, 2136.
Interurban highways, 2170–2211.
Interurban street-railways. 2350.
  (Terminals), (2780).
Iron and steel (Buildings), 3528.
Irrigation (Soil), 4844.
Irrigation canals, Streets with, 2118.
Island cities (Types of plans), 5260.
Island reservations, 4184.
Islands (Topographical data), 1372.
Isles of safety, 2128.

J

Jetties (Protective works), 2617.
Jetties, wharves, piers, etc., 2680–2729.
Junctions, Street, 2135–2138.

INDEX

INDEX

Lots (*continued*)
Subdivision of blocks into, 3160–3163.
Topography, 3293–3295.
Low areas, Filling of, 1347.
Low-cost multiple houses in-block, 3644.
Low-cost residential districts. 1697.
Low-cost semi-detached houses, 3659.
Low-cost single detached houses, 3654.
Low-cost single houses in-block, 3639.
Lumber, Areas for handling and storing (Waterfronts), 2723.
Lumber-yards, 3197.

M

Maintenance, *see* Construction and maintenance.
Maps, 834.
Malls, 2258.
Man-hole covers, 2124, (2306).
Manufacturing, Buildings for, 3595.
Manufacturing cities (Types of plans), 5321.
Manufacturing districts, 1650.
Manufacturing plants, 3195.
Utilization of waterfront by, 2740.
Manuscripts (General collections), 292
Marine parks, 4181.
Market districts, 1660.
Market-garden areas, 1723.
Market places, 4425.
Market squares, 4425.
Markets.
(Buildings), 3610.
Relation to terminal facilities, 2827.
Marquees (Encroachment on streets), 2159.
Marshes (Topographical data), 1352.
Materials, Building, 3510–3539.
Types of city plans distinguished by, 5680.
Materials, Structural, 3520–3529.
Mediaeval cities, 225.
Medium-cost multiple houses in-block, 3643.
Medium-cost residential districts, 1696.
Medium-cost semi-detached houses, 3658.
Medium-cost single detached houses, 3653.

Medium-cost single houses in-block, 3638.
Medium-sized cities (Types of plans), 5615.
Methods of technical procedure. Professional practice, 800–880.
Military cities (Types of plans), 5311.
Mills, 3595.
Mineral wealth (Data), 1557.
Mining cities (Types of plans), 5322.
Minor buildings, 3670–3689.
Minor streets, Location, 1820.
Minor structures, 3820–3885.
Model housing, 1432–1433.
Models, 836, 856.
Modern cities, 230.
Monumental arches, 3830.
Monumental squares, 4435, (4575).
Monumental statues, 3840.
Monuments, 3830.
Motor traffic, Influence on streets, 2058.
Motor trucks (Data), 2076.
Movement, City-planning, 500–(600).
Multiple houses in-block, 3641–3644.
Multiple streets, 2115.
Municipal, *Cf.* City, *and also* second words of certain phrases beginning with municipal, *e. g.*, Municipal nurseries, *see* Nurseries.
Municipal art, 1235.
Municipal buildings, 3563–3568.
Municipal engineering, *see* Conduits. Wires; Public health and safety; Sewage disposal; Streets, roads. Footways; Water-supply.
Municipal finances (Data), 1570–1595.
Municipal government, *see* 714, 1225, 1525–1540.
Municipal improvement (Term), 300.
Municipal improvement movement, 500–(600).
Municipal model housing, 1432.
Municipal services.
Buildings for, 3568.
Open spaces devoted to operation of, 4500–4549.
Museums, (70)–85.
(Buildings), 3570.

INDEX

Recreation, Public (Data), 1495.
Recreation areas, Distribution, 1730.
Recreation piers, 4199.
Recreational building groups, 3728.
Recreational waterfronts, 4170–4205.
Rectilinear type of informal plat, 1847.
(Types of city plans), 5647.
Redistribution of land, 728.
Refreshment places, 4139.
Refuse disposal, 1472.
Regulations, (765).
As subdivision of special subjects,
see Legislation.
Reinforced concrete, 3527.
Replanning, 1200–1851.
Burned districts, 1617.
Reports, 832–852.
Requirements of city planning as
an art, science, or profession,
322.
Reservations, 4150–4230.
Corners, 3183.
(Separate roadways), (2109).
Street-railway, 2382.
Reservations and parks, 4100–4290.
Reservoir reservations, 4210.
Reservoirs, 4510.
Residences, 3620–3669.
See also Houses.
Residential blocks (Areas), 3230–3240.
Residential cities (Types of plans),
5330–5333.
Residential districts, 1676–1708.
Residential lots, 3380–3395.
Residential squares, 2238, (4445).
Residential streets, 2235–2238.
Planting, 4892.
Resorts, Health and pleasure (Types
of plans), 5333.
Resources.
Economic and financial (Data),
1545–1595.
Natural (Data), 1557.
Resting places, (Parks, etc.), 4137.
Restrictions.
Affecting appearance of buildings,
3460.
(Blocks and lots), 3020.
Retail districts, 1670.
Retail shops, 3600.
Blocks occupied by, 3210.
Revenue service quarters, 2690.

Revision and amplification of city
plans, 846.
Rights-of-way.
Creation 735.
(Railroad), 2500–2504.
Rights, Laws relating to.
Private, 1515.
Public, 1510.
Ringstrassen, 2183.
River bank reservations, 4183.
River cities (Types of plans), 5265.
Rivers.
(Commercial waterways), 2580–
(2595).
(Topographical data), 1376.
Roads, 2050–2328.
Roadside improvement, 4875–4893.
(Roadways, Separate), (2107).
Rock (Soil), 1382.
Roof gardens, 4919.
Roofs, 3504.
Round-point and radius type of plat,
1841.
(Types of city plans), 5641.
Round-points, 2197.
Routes, Determining location of main
thoroughfares, 1814.
Rubbish disposal, 1472.
Running tracks, 4370.
Rural improvement movement, 584.

S

Safety, Isles of, 2128.
Sand (Soil), 1382.
Sanitation, see Public health and
safety, 1445–1485.
Scale, in general effect of buildings,
3455.
Scales, City, 3872.
School gardens, 4907.
Schools.
(Buildings), 3570.
(For study and teaching of city
planning), 980–998.
Schools, Public, Teaching of city
planning in, 548.
Seacoast (Topographical data), 1370.
Seashore reservations, 4181.
Seats, 3860.
Sea walls, 2619.
Semi-detached houses, 3656–3659.
Districts with, 1707.

97

INDEX

INDEX

INDEX

INDEX

INDEX

INDEX

Y

Yards.
 Brick, 3197.
 Freight (Railroad), 2495.
 Lumber, 3197.
 Municipal, 4540.
 Stock, 3197.
 Street-railway, 2420.

Tan, 3197.
Train, 2490.
Yearbooks, 15.

Z

Zoning, 1620.
Zoölogical parks, 4270.

Z 697
C 53 P 8
1913

Lightning Source UK Ltd.
Milton Keynes UK
UKHW021137100119
335177UK00006B/621/P